THUGGED OUT

Apostle Carolyn Edwards

© 2013, Carolyn Edwards. All Rights Reserved.

No part of this publication may be reproduced or transmitted in any form or by any means, electronic or mechanical, including photocopy, recording, or any information storage and retrieval systems, without written permission from the publisher, except in the case of brief quotations embodied in critical articles and reviews.

Printed in the United States of America.

ISBN: 0615833527
ISBN-13: 978-0615833521

Published & Distributed By:
Doors of Life

Introduction

Thugged out Christians are people who came from the dark side and the streets. God gave these individuals another chance at life (God is the potter and we are the clay). The lord molded and made us into the person he wants us to become. Most of our problems are, when God is molding and making us, we jump out of the creator's hands and find a fake pair of hands to shape us. Upon completion of the body shaping assignment, we get mad and wonder why our body is messed up. The first thing we need to admit to ourselves is that we tried to copy God's creation - the word lets us know, we do not think like God or have the Lord's mind. Now your process of being molded and made has to start all over again, if you want the body God has designed for you.

Thugged Out also means: I have hit rock bottom, died on the operating table, bullet just missed my head and the prison food that I eat on a daily basis is passing right through me - Saints of God, we have to be delivered from everything and we need to be skilled on all levels of ministry, before we try to cast a 'thug demon' out of someone. God will heal and clean us up then God will send some of us back to the street to pull broken people out of the same garbage can he pulled us out of. Be it known, if there are any stones left unturned on the inward part of you, these spirits will consume you to the point of no return.

Chapter 1
Thugged Out

Have you ever been to a place in your life where you wanted to walk away from everything? Marriage on the rocks, children out of control, friends have turned their backs on you, next you lose your only source of income - it feels like God isn't listening or answering your prayers - Then you fall for the first thing that makes you smile… You don't even have to be happy, just the mere fact that something or somebody paid you some attention, at this time in your life. We talk a lot about faith but we never use it in the time of need.

Its funny how we look for something or someone to help us come out of our funk (attitude, depression, loneliness, hurt and pain), we do not even stop and think about the problem. Check this out, we don't even listen or look for the solution - we just start trying different things to see if it'll make us tick (arouse or wake something up in us). When was the last time you gave yourself a compliment without finding fault within your own self? All your life people (family included) have found something wrong with you - now the enemy doesn't even have to beat us down; we do it enough to our self.

Look at this illustration the Lord shared with me - One day you wake up and find yourself in a courtroom. You are the judge, jury and the defendant; some of us are messed up to the point we'll even sentence ourselves time in prison. Many of God's people might not understand this knowledge (but it is a mind thing). The enemy knows that the mind is a playground of trials and tribulation. As long as the devil can keep our focus on our issues, he never has to worry about us leading anyone into the kingdom of God to be delivered and set free. Isaiah 40:30-31 "Those who hope in the Lord will renew their strength. They will soar on wings like eagles; they will run and not grow weary, they will run and not be faint." I hear a lot of preachers say an idle mind is the devil's workshop.

Let's tap into some thugged out people in the Bible… In Second Samuel, Absalom had a lovely sister; whose name was Tamar and Amnon the son of David loved her. So Jonadab King David's brother's son said to him, " Lie down on your bed and pretend to be ill. And when your father comes to see you, say to him, 'Please let my sister Tamar come and give me food, and prepare the food in my sight, that I might see it and eat it from her hand." King David sent his daughter Tamar to Amnon's

house to cook food for him. King David being a man after God on heart had no discernment. He sent his daughter into the devil's den wild - How many of us were set up by our own parents?!
Tamar took the cakes she made for her step-brother into his bedroom, Amnon took hold of her, and said to her, "Come, lie with me my sister." She said, "No my brother, do not force me," however he would not heed to her voice; and being stronger than she, he forced her and lay with her. Amnon hated her exceedingly, so that the hatred with which he hated her was greater than the love he had for her. Anyway, Tamar had no idea her virginity would be taking away from her that day by her thugged out step-brother.

Houston, we have a problem! Tamar's brother took something (innocence) from her that he can never give back. Now Tamar is wounded, ashamed, abandonment and all alone. Later in Second Samuel we read that Tamar put ashes on her head, and tore her robe of many colors that was on her, and laid her hands on her head and went away crying bitterly. Absalom, her brother spoke to Amnon neither good nor bad; for Absalom hated Amnon, because he had forced his sister Tamar. And it came to pass, after two full years, Absalom had sheepshearers in Baal Hazor, which is near Ephraim; so Absalom invited all the king's sons. Now Absalom had commanded his servants, saying, watch now, when Amnon's heart is merry with wine, and when I say to you, Strike Amnon! Then kill him. Do not be afraid. Have I not commanded you? Be courageous and valiant. So the servant of Absalom did to Amnon as Absalom had commanded. Then all of the King's sons arose, and each one got on his mule and fled.

Saints of God, please be aware of the enemy's games and devices he uses on us to shift our focus. Absalom was a King's kid with many brothers and sisters who he loved. One day the devil saw an opening to destroy the man of God's family, but hold up wait a minute, King David bought this curse into his own blood line - by killing a man and taking the man's wife for himself. Don't get this thing twisted, I do not care how long you've been saved, sanctified, Holy Ghost fill and fire baptized we all have moments. Jesus had a moment in the garden of Gethsemane he said "Father if it be thy will, pass this cup from me." I promise you baby, don't mess with me in my moment (attitude all over the place, let go and let God shake me back, if you do it – Houston, we are going to have a problem).

The old people used to say "Mama's baby, Daddy's maybe." If this shoe hit you, go in your closet and tell God about it - please do not let this pain sidetrack you from your given destination. I am not telling you to act like a donkey (*okay – ass*) Now can we move with the knowledge God is down loading in us.

Apostle Edwards came from the streets, so I am not trying to be your best friend - I just want to give you a reality check. My best friend in this whole world dropped me like a hot potato, for a boy wearing grown-men pants. I was heartbroken. I used to fight for her in elementary school because all the other children use to pick on her but any way that's another book. Every day after I lost my best friend, I began to ask myself what I did wrong. As young as I was, God began to talk to me about trying to pull people with me that were no longer my assignment. Boom got me! So I asked God to remove the pain and fill the void in my heart. That was a gold nugget you need to file in your mind.

Writing this book takes me back to a subject called "loyalty" - This is how so many of our thugged out children die in them streets; watching somebody's back. These are the new heroes of the streets that some of our young people look up to like drug dealers, thieves, murderers, pimps, prostitutes, etc. In the old days our heroes were pastors, fathers, mothers, teachers, mothers of the church, Superman, Batman, He-man, and please do not forget Wonder Woman. Okay, let me move own from my past and let's talk more about loyalty - 2 Chronicles 18:3- 9; 12- 22 - so, Ahab king of Israel asked Jehoshaphat king of Judah, "Will you go with me against Ramoth Gilead?" Jehoshaphat replied, "I am as you are, and my people as your people; we will join you in the war." *Comment: why in the hill side would you go to a war that you have nothing to do with? It's called loyalty.*

But Jehoshaphat also said to the king of Israel, "First seek the counsel of the LORD." So the king of Israel brought together the prophets—four hundred men—and asked them, "Shall we go to war against Ramoth Gilead, or shall I not?" "Go," they answered, "for God will give it into the king's hand." But Jehoshaphat asked, "Is there no longer a prophet of the LORD here whom we can inquire of?" *Comment: If four hundred people say go, whose side would you be on? You lie - we always say everybody 'aint going to tell the same lie- got you Boo!*

The king of Israel answered Jehoshaphat, "There is still one prophet through whom we can inquire of the LORD, but I hate him because he never prophesies anything good about me, but always bad. He is

Micaiah son of Imlah." "The king should not say such a thing," Jehoshaphat replied. So the king of Israel called one of his officials and said, "Bring Micaiah son of Imlah at once." Dressed in their royal robes, the king of Israel and Jehoshaphat king of Judah were sitting on their thrones at the threshing floor by the entrance of the gate of Samaria, with all the prophets prophesying before them. *Comment: If you know the prophets are not real, why in hillside would you allow them to speak words over your life?*

And the messenger that went to call Micaiah spake to him, saying, Behold, the words of the prophets declare good to the king with one assent; let thy word therefore, I pray thee, be like one of their's, and speak thou good. And Micaiah said, As the LORD liveth, even what my God saith, that will I speak. And when he was come to the king, the king said unto him, Micaiah, shall we go to Ramothgilead to battle, or shall I forbear? And he said, Go ye up, and prosper, and they shall be delivered into your hand. And the king said to him, How many times shall I adjure thee that thou say nothing but the truth to me in the name of the LORD? Then he said, I did see all Israel scattered upon the mountains, as sheep that have no shepherd: and the LORD said, These have no master; let them return therefore every man to his house in peace. And the king of Israel said to

Jehoshaphat, Did I not tell thee that he would not prophesy good unto me, but evil?

Again he said, Therefore hear the word of the LORD; I saw the LORD sitting upon his throne, and all the host of heaven standing on his right hand and on his left. And the LORD said, Who shall entice Ahab king of Israel, that he may go up and fall at Ramothgilead? And one spake saying after this manner, and another saying after that manner. Then there came out a spirit, and stood before the LORD, and said, I will entice him. And the LORD said unto him, Wherewith? And he said, I will go out, and be a lying spirit in the mouth of all his prophets. And the Lord said, Thou shalt entice him, and thou shalt also prevail: go out, and do even so. Now therefore, behold, the LORD hath put a lying spirit in the mouth of these thy prophets, and the LORD hath spoken evil against thee.

2 Chronicles 18:26-29 - And say, Thus says the king put this fellow in prison, and feed him with bread of affliction, until I return in peace. And Micaiah said, if you ever return in peace, then had not the Lord has not spoken by me. And he said, Hearken, all you people! *Just one comment right here*, Micaiah stated to King Ahab why did you send for me, if you did not want to know the truth? (I was at my own home

chilling, sipping on some Kool-Aid, watching T.V. - Your messenger you sent disturbed me. But trying to do the right thing, I came to see what you wanted. Now you want to lock me up in prison for telling you the truth, hail to the king.

Now check this out: 2 Chronicles 18:29-32 - And the king of Israel said unto Jehoshaphat, I will disguise myself, and I will go to the battle; but put thou on thy robes. So the king of Israel disguised himself; and they went to the battle. Now the king of Syria had commanded the captains of the chariots that were with him, saying, Fight ye not with small or great, save only with the king of Israel. And it came to pass, when the captains of the chariots saw Jehoshaphat, that they said, It is the king of Israel. Therefore they compassed about him to fight: but Jehoshaphat cried out, and the LORD helped him; and God moved them to depart from him. For it came to pass, that, when the captains of the chariots perceived that it was not the king of Israel, they turned back again from pursuing him. *Comment: Baby, Jehoshaphat got that thing twisted! How do you allow your loyalty to put you in a death burial situation? God showed you on several occasions your boy was setting you up for the okie-doke. But your loyalty would not allow you to abort this assignment after the Lord told you to get out while you still have a chance, with your want to be thugged out self.*

Houston we have a problem! You were willing to die for this demon but as soon as the men from the other side landed on your head to cut it off, you did what all the people do when they are on their way out - he cried out for God's to help him. The Lord heard his voice and came to his rescue. To God be the Glory, when a real prophet gives you a word from the Lord you better take heed of the word and not allow the word to fall on the ground. The prophet Micaiah told King Ahab he would be killed in the battle at Ramoth-Gilead. King Ahab's four-hundred false prophets told him to go to war and he would come back, the king had no insight or discernment that this was a set up from the pit of hell. God's prophet told the king he was going to die, but the king had so much pride and anger towards the man of God, he would not listen.

2 Chronicles 28:33-34 - And a certain man drew a bow at a venture, and smote the king of Israel between the joints of the harness: therefore he said to his chariot man, Turn thine hand, that thou mayest carry me out of the host; for I am wounded. And the battle increased that day: howbeit the king of Israel stayed himself up in his chariot against the Syrians

until the even: and about the time of the sun going down he died.

Church people put John on the land of Patmos. They wanted John the revelator to die, hoping the people on that land would kill him, but God gave him revelation and knowledge to share with the saints. People of the most high, God gave us the road map that we should follow on this journey. Have you ever seen people in church playing with their cell phone while the preacher is ministering a sermon? They have no clue the enemy has taken control of their focus. God gave us the blueprint we should follow to heaven, but if you do not want to complete your God giving destination, do not blame anyone but yourself when you wake up in hell realizing you had a thugged out mentality. If you believe in your heart and confess with your mouth that Jesus died on the cross you are saved. It you believe God raised Jesus up on the third day you are saved. Once you receive God in your heart and mind, your thugged out decision making will change from negative to positive due to the new nature in you from God.

Chapter 2
Kicked Out Of The Church

Growing up as a child I lived in the church house due to my mother finding God for real, in her renewed sanctify soul, in a small Holy Ghost church. Being a child with a lot of mouth and a hard head, I thought the Lord was punishing me by allowing my mother to stay in church all day. She was the one who found God - I was not looking for the Lord, Jesus or the Holy Spirit. Nevertheless, I was told by my mother to love someone or something I could not see nor talk to but I could feel something down in my spirit man. My mother, Mary, stated God was her everything.

Now check this out, I began to look for my mother's new boyfriend but he never came around when I was awake. But every night I would hear my mother talking to her new boyfriend and he would make her cry, then she would laugh - next I would hear strange words that didn't make sense to me. I could not ask her what was going on in her bedroom because I was supposed to be sleeping. My mother began to sanctify her mind, body and soul, she fasted 4 to 5 times per week and all you could hear throughout the house was Jesus, Jesus, and Jesus. You have no idea how my life changed overnight. I began to hate church, people of God please explain to your children about the Lord. If you do not know anything about the Lord please find a real person in God that is saved, sanctified and filled with God Holy Ghost. Remember men and women of the most high God - a demon knows a demon, and a demon knows a real saint.

Baby, a lot of us got this thing twisted - my mom went from smoking 3 packs of cigarettes a day to praying 3-4 times a day. Then she stopped dressing like a diva and began to sanctify herself. I remember the day she gave all her diva clothing away (fitted pants, hot and sexy tops, the bomb underwear and so much more). Mary had found something in God that made her want to get rid of everything she thought was nasty and dirty. Mary wanted to clean her body up from past hurts, disappointment, let downs and relationships. The butt-naked truth is, Mary accepted the Lord and savior Jesus Christ as her everything. As time went on the woman of God fell deeper and deeper in God.

Okay here we go - Mary started having an Acts 6:8-13 experience - And Stephen, full of faith and power, did great wonders and miracles among the people. Then there arose certain of the synagogue, which is called the synagogue of the Libertines, and Cyrenians, and Alexandrians, and of them of Cilicia and of Asia, disputing with Stephen. And they were not able to resist the wisdom and the spirit by which he spake. Then they suborned men, which said, We have heard him speak blasphemous words against Moses, and against God. And they stirred up the people, and the elders, and the scribes, and came upon him, and caught him, and brought him to the council, and set up false witnesses, which said, This man ceaseth not to speak blasphemous words against this holy place, and the law:

Now check this out, Mary left the street life alone because, she found God and his wonder working power. This strength she received from the Lord fulfilled her everything (mind, body and soul). Mary thought everything in life was going to be better for her and her children. Baby she got that thing twisted; once you find out, Philippians 4:13 - *I can do all things through Christ who strengthens me*) - her new life in the church was turning out to be worse than her street life. Mary got turned out from the church people but she stayed with her God. You must be able to stand alone in this generation of so-called saints of God. They will shout with you, cry with you, pray for you and stab you in the heart with a smile on their face as if they are doing you a favor.

Houston we have a problem - this is the appointed time to see if you have changed for real in life.

I used to be an alley cat but now I am a lady for the kingdom of God. Boom got you together quickly, let us move on with the knowledge God is down loading in us - One thing I always think about is how the mother of Jesus (Mary) was filled twice with the Holy Ghost - Once in Luke 1:41- And it came to pass, that, when Elisabeth heard the salutation of Mary, the babe leaped in her womb; and Elisabeth was filled with the Holy Ghost. Then Acts 1:14 - These all continued with one accord in prayer and supplication, with the women, and Mary the mother of Jesus, and with his brethren. Acts 2:2-4 - And suddenly there came a sound from heaven as of a rushing mighty wind, and it filled all the house where they were sitting. And there appeared unto them cloven tongues like as of fire, and it sat upon each of them. And they were all filled with the Holy Ghost, and began to speak with other tongues, as the Spirit gave them utterance.

We might be thugged out but God loves his messed up children too. The Lord has no respect of person. Have you ever been in church and when the door opened everybody in church turns around to see who just came in the door? The enemy has stolen everybody's focus unaware. God loves the broken hearted and the backslider.

The church people send the backslidden, broken hearted, abused, molested, and mentally challenged people back to the street. This is why you yourself have to know, God renews your mind, then changes your way of thinking and life forever. Now, you sit in front of the church instead of by the back by the door. The word says watch as well as pray, because you can be caught up in someone at church and they come at you with the wrong spirit and the old you rises up for the occasion - that is God's way of letting you know it is still some stuff in there. What we need to recognize at that moment is that the spirit in them rose up at you to bring you out of retirement - do not let the devil see you sweat. Satan does not have new tricks he just uses different faces to knock you off your square. Most of the time it is somebody in a church position who is supposed to be filled with the Holy Ghost. Baby, please don't get that thing twisted, a lot of people attend and play church - this does not mean they are filled with the Holy Ghost.

We as people of the Lord must fast and pray and give God his ten percent of our time on a daily bases. A lot of Christian feels like they pay their tithe money that should be enough; the God I serve demands ten percent of everything we have obtained and own. Let me make this plan for you - your husband, children, family, money, house, car, job, and everything else I forgot to say. After your fasting and praying then you can get the discernment, you need on the inside so you can see deeper than the face value and smile of an individual. Saints of the highest God - never put your trust in flesh; the Bible states there is nothing good in your flesh.

I remember when I first moved to Chicago. I met two prophets and they took me to lunch one day; it was so nice until we left. Both of the women of God went off on me and this blew my wig back! Carolyn Ann rose up for the occasion. But God, caught my tongue - you know I was fend to catch a case (street people you know what I mean, "open up a can of whoop ass - I am sorry if this is too street for some of y'all sanctified folks, just do a quick shout and get over it).

Please people of the most high God, remember one thing, this book is for the *thugged out* saints who got out of them streets alive. I know you are still struggling with some issues the key to this is to keep everything real to yourself and spouse - such as if you used to be gay, tell them you had some cross the water experience - if they are mature they are going to be hurt, broken, and very pissed off. So do yourself a favor and be up front about your past relationships, habits, problems and everything else you can think of - if they cannot handle it I promise you one thing, God always keeps a ram in the bush for his children. People of God remember whatever you do in the dark it will show up in your light and life at the wrong time. Satan always waits on the perfect moment to put you on blast in front of the world to the point of no return.

Chapter 3
Street Life Is Killing Me

Now at this time in my life, the streets are killing me - everything I have done is right before me in this court of law. My mind keeps going over the people I have robbed, killed, sold drugs - I didn't care about anything in my life. I had lost my daddy in them streets. I lost my mother to the streets (drugs and prostitution). I made my money off everybody - I had nothing to lose; I fed the minor children whose parents were hooked on crack cocaine and alcohol. Once they made ten years old, I began to teach them the rules and regulations of the street.

I know you think I am a bad person because I accepted the addict's food stamps and their paychecks but what you did not know is I took care of their children and all the abandoned street children. Oh my God, so many young girls I tried to send back home from them streets but they would not listen to me and go back home. They felt like street life was much better than being back at home with a nagging mother and an abusive father. Therefore, I took their virginity and put them to work on the street for me, if I had not done this to those young girls they would be somebody else's (a pimp's) property. Now they are no longer my friends, they are now my workhorses. I own each one of them now - they do not get retirement; they died out.

Please remember church people, I do not trust anybody. My whole family came out of those streets. My father was a chief over the drugs game and he had a lot of followers in those streets. He even got respect from the police – 'aint that a trip? My father came up in the civil rights movement when the colored people were being mistreated. He made himself a promise - no one will ever take him down. Yes, he knew his way of thinking was wrong but he refused to let his father and forefathers down. This young man was only sixteen years old but all he knew was street life. He was proud to be a thug. This young man had watched his father feed a whole community. Then his daddy took care of his runner's (work boy's) family while, they were in the pin for selling his product on the street. These men treated my family like royalty, my father was a good man but he had his shortcomings and faults like everyone else that came from street life.

I always think about King David, in Psalm 51:3-5 - For I acknowledge my transgressions: and my sin is ever before me. Against thee, thee only, have I sinned, and done this evil in thy sight: that thou mightest be justified when thou speakest, and be clear when thou judgest. Behold, I was shapen in iniquity; and in sin did my mother conceive me.

This generation of young people need to know where they came from. Back in the day, we used to hear children saying that wanted to be like Pastor So-n-so, but now they want to be a drug dealer, thugged out - these young people really just want somebody to love them for real. Most pastors, preachers, prophets, are not fit to be a role model to anyone. Their life is not blameless, they will cuss you out at the drop of a dime. James 3:10 - Out of the same mouth proceedeth blessing and cursing. My brethren, these things ought not so to be.

My father never had a lot of time for me because he was running the family empire. Many people were shot up, protecting my daddy in those streets. My uncle was a gang banger and my father's number one bodyguard, he had much respect from the hood-rats, and dope addicted, killers, young and old G's. Respect was not giving to anyone in those streets, you had to earn it.

As I sat in the courtroom listening to all, the charges they had on me - thinking I am going to spend the rest of my life in prison. Please remember saints of God, God has the last say, grace and mercy always shows up when sin is in the camp.

I remember one Christmas day my father came through the front door bearing gifts for the family. I was so excited to see what he had bought for me - I had a beautiful bike, trains sets, race cars - I had everything a child could want. Well later on that day my father lost his life trying to help a cracked out woman on Christmas day get something to eat. This woman was living on the streets and had no family. That same day my mother and I died and went to hell with my father. For the first time in my life I understand the movie "The Walking Dead." My plans of becoming somebody great (teacher, firefighter, college graduate, and owning my own auto body shop) in this world was lost forever.

Now I remember what happened to me while sitting in this courtroom awaiting - my uncle was a thugged out gang banger in those streets. He raised me and taught me everything he knew about them streets. At the age of 15, I killed my first man. It did not even hurt me I was numb down to the bone. I was hurting so bad on the inside of me, every time I saw a cracked out female, it was on I would make her pay for my father's life repeatedly until I was tired. I had to become a thug because my father and his family were thugged out. I never wanted my family and friends to call me a punk, the men in my family were good stock soldiers (grade a beef). I was always told if you do the crime, you need to do your time. My father and the men I looked up to all my life made it through prison, so can I.

Nevertheless, once I was arrested on a Friday night around 2am, my entire posse (boys) left me standing alone - holding the bag of crack rock cocaine, true that, it was my dope so I took all the blame. I never knew the devil had placed a hit out on the men in my family until I found The Lord in a prison cell for real.

I have been to a lot of churches but I could always see straight through the so-called ministry team. When most of the young church woman found out I had money, they dropped them draws quicker than a prostitute does. Stop tripping, you have not been out of the garbage can that long, with your want to be so sanctified self. I got to keep this new found knowledge real to myself, life took a turn for me when I tried God at his word, for myself. God protected me and gave me favor with the judge. I only got five years - served two in prison and the other three years on paper with a parole officer on my back. I have finished serving all my time and I am finally free with a degree in auto body - everything is lovely. Now I am a thug for the highest God.

Chapter 4
Thugged Out Female

These are females who have been broken, raped, beat on a daily basis, abandoned, rejected, and need to be in control of everybody's situation they come in contact with. The first challenge of life is we must understand Revelation 2:20 - Notwithstanding I have a few things against thee, because thou sufferest that woman Jezebel, which calleth herself a prophetess, to teach and to seduce my servants to commit fornication, and to eat things sacrificed unto idols.

The spirit of Jezebel is rebellious, controlling, manipulative, unbridled witchcraft, hatred for male authority and sexual perversity. Jezebel targets women who are embittered against men either through neglect or misuse of authority. This spirit operates through women who, because of insecurity, jealousy or vanity, desire to control and dominate others. She is behind the woman who publicly humiliates her husband with her tongue and then thereafter controls him by his fears of public embarrassment. There are good women who come to the church seeking God, but this spirit has them fantasizing about the men in this assembly—lamenting that their husbands are not as spiritual as other husbands.

I have met many women in this generation that have been thugged out. For instance, I met a pastor in New York City that blew my hair back. Bishop and I were conducting a meeting with some new pastors that came up under our umbrella (church). I asked the ladies in the room one question - How many men have you been with sexually up to this day? I know you see many people attending church, that doesn't mean everybody is coming to be saved, delivered, set free or filled with the Holy Ghost. I have met a lot of lay members having sex with the church people, starting at the pulpit to the back door.

Would you like to know where thugged out women come from? A lot of them are these hurt little girls where their father has abused and molested (raped) them mentally and physically (Lot's daughters got him drunk and they had sex with him). There are many dads whom feel like they have a right to lay with their children. See how stupid the devil makes people act and you wonder why so many older women are messed up today?! These people never got a real deliverance from their pain, the parents of these children never talk about the abuse that went on in their home - no apology/forgiveness was made to these broken children and they turn away from truth. These men come home drunk getting in the wrong beds. I was always told by the older women 'a drunken man always speaks his true feeling and does what has been playing in their mind like a rerun.' The alcohol only gives them the courage to do what they have been dreaming about all the time.

Have you ever been in a room with family and you get that nasty feeling in your soul, than they come by you and touch you improperly and you will get chills all over your little body? What happens next to you has always pissed me off - I am sorry if the words 'pissed off' mess with your Holy Ghost, if so - get over it. If you have never been violated by a family member, mother's boyfriend or close supposed to be friend of your family you will never understand freedom, these words I am trying to share with you are from my past pain.

God is the key and I can promise you Giants do come down. Do not allow the devil to punk you out of your mind - you refuse to let your past go and all you think about is the rerun that the enemy keeps showing you in your mind. One question please, if you could not get over the abuse from whatever source the enemy used to destroy your life, how in the hell did you become a prostitute? Oh hold up wait a minute, you became the one thing that caused you the most pain. Can you tell me how did you allow that to happen? Do you know by now the devil's job is to kill, steal and destroy? What did Satan say to you that made you not eat, sleep, feel or know any kind of emotion and give up on life? But you got married to somebody that saw something in you worth fighting for - the problem is you never allow the Lord to make you all over again (whole).

Now the children that were conceived from a thugged out female, downloaded rejection, abandonment, and depression into her helpless fetus. Now check this out a newborn baby is already tore up from the floor up. Psalm 51:5 - Behold, I was shapen in iniquity; and in sin did my mother conceive me.

I came here knowing how to lie, turn a trick, rob people and kill anything I wanted to. The dark side was already in my mind, body, and soul. Now your children got to deal with an alcoholic and drug addict for a mother - you can always get help, the only problem you might have is coming across someone just like you. Whenever you come up out of the garbage can, you will always have a follower who wants to bring you back out of retirement. The old saying is 'misery loves company' - we have a lot of sisters that turn to the streets to make themselves a real and true family because the one God place them in was defective. God will put us in rough places to make our ministry. Men and women of God you can only minister to what you were in the streets. And for the Mary Poppins (pure women) generation that never did anything in them streets - to God be the Glory. Stop acting like you were born in the church, we all know about the thugged out loose women, homosexual, liars, back biters, mess starters and so on always up in somebody's face. Go back a couple years when you were in those street and remember what people used to say about you being thugged out. Then take your life from there and say thank you to the Lord.

Chapter 5
Thugged Out Teenagers

Our children, in this old wicked society and perverse generation, have no love in their hearts. These children will kill at will and have no remorse about the crime they have done. I remember in the past, everybody wanted to be a pastor, firefighter, or police offers. These men have disappointed so many children by leaving home - see a lot of men get this saying wrong, I don't care if the relationship went bad with your child mother the baby never ask you to come here. Even if she is trifling and out of order your child needs you to interfere in their little life - fight for your baby. The enemy is always going to show you, you and most of us do not like what we see.

I remember always-asking God to take the excess weight off me, God replied to me saying "I did not lift your hands to your mouth." God also stated, fasting and praying will always pull off strongholds - the key is you have to want to be released from bondage. People of God, we have to take our children back from these streets, we have to first fall back in love with ourselves look at fear and pain in the mirror, stand up to the devil and let him know - I am taking my life, husband, children, finances, and health back. I have toted you long enough and to my wicked family that have broken me down to the morrow of my bone to the point of no return that do not want Christ in your life 'See ya don't not want to be ya!' Boom got you.

People please help me teach our children how to love themselves past the pain they have experienced from rejection, abandonment, abuse mentally and physically and molestation - it is ok to tell someone now, baby. I do not care if they believe you or not, nevertheless it is time for you to live and be free. People of old times have always protected the wrong person (family) so you can be free and live again. Many of our babies turn into a predator (wicked people) to survive on the streets because they refuse to go back to a place where they are not wanted. Yes, I know a lot of our children lie and we need to teach them a lesson, but at what cost? Most of us ran our babies away because we never got a real deliverance from our own parents.

Many of our parents were abused mentally and physically, they were told by your grandparents to keep their mouth shut and that is the mentality of our mothers and grandmothers. How many of your mothers watch her man rape you and acted like nothing ever happened? I have worked in my past with mothers that were hooked on drugs and sold their daughter virginity to get them a fix. Can you image being raped, touch improperly or beat because your mother's boyfriend wanted you instead of your mama? A lot of them were abused worse than we could ever imagine. Let us have a moment of silence for all the people in bondage due to the hurt they experienced from their parents - thank you God.

On this journey called life I had to forgive family and friends for disrespecting my intelligence by mistreating me in every way you can imagine. Never think because you are tired the enemy will stop picking at you. David was a young boy when his ministry first started - this position might not look powerful but you have to go through training and battle before you can lead anyone. Saints, remember satan and God are always looking for worship to build up their kingdom.

Chapter 6
Thugged Out Babies

These millennium babies (born in the year 2000 and up to this present day) are thugged out with a mindset of doing their own things. Control, to these babies, is a form of abuse in every area. They do not follow direction, slow to answer you back, throw all their things on the floor, lie, steal, and hate school. Check this out - these babies do not like sleep, most of them stay constipated and they have a problem with authority figures. Our toddlers are in trouble - their future is hanging in some of these so-called parents' hands. Calling all intercession to stand in the gap for our babies and break the curses off of their little lives.

Chapter 7
Hit Rock Bottom

I have lost everything - family, children, job, my mind, body and soul. I am on the verge of taking my own life. No one wants to be bothered with me. The enemy told me if I acted a fool everybody would pay me some attention. My life took a turn for the worse - I hit them streets hard. I began to rob everybody and killing became my second nature. I was thugged out and it felt so good - everyone knew my name in them streets so I went deeper in the game called life. I began to steal, sell drugs, buy property - the money came to me like rain falling from the sky. Women asked me to be their pimp - the doors were opening up to bigger and better things. To me, my empire was growing bigger - nobody could tell me what to do any more. My emotions were out of control. Satan had hooked me like a fish and I fell for the okie-doke.

Chapter 8
Producing the Promise Through Your Seed

Luke 8:11 - Now the parable is this: The seed is the word of God.

1) A seed contains life and is powerful (God is the light of the world).
2) A seed does nothing until it is planted (a seed has to die before it can reproduce).
3) A seed always produces after its own kind (we should be producing fruit in God's image).
4) A seed grows in secret (underground), (what you do in secret, God will reward you openly).
5) A seed is not infected by other seeds (but a seed can hop on an individual, be careful of the people you hang around - spirits are transferable).
6) A seed needs water/nourishment (word of God) or it will not grow (Jesus cursed a fig tree that had not produced fruit in its season).
7) A seed is persistent (the seed of God will never stop producing fruit of its kind).

Steps to Reaching Your Promise

Hebrews 6:12 - That ye be not slothful, but followers of them who through faith and patience inherit the promises.

1) Pick fertile ground to plant your seed.
2) Clear the debris out of the soil to make the dirt rich.
3) Dig and plow your own field.
4) Put your seed in the ground.
5) Water your garden daily.
6) Add mulch to your garden (mulch keeps weeds out and the word of God in the rich soil).
7) Pray over your harvest daily.

Chapter 9
Conclusion

The enemy's job is to always stop God's people from completing their destination and brining more souls into the kingdom of God. Paul and Silas went to a city to attend prayer but they ran in to a damsel with the spirit of divination, which grieved Paul.

The first thing I have to admit to myself is - I was thugged out. Saints of the most High God, can I keep this thing real? See, I cannot go to a church were the pastor teaches a, b, c nursery rhymes. I demand the pure unadulterated gospel - this is the only thing I know will keep me out of those streets. Please understand me, I was not born that way - I was made that way by life, abuse, rejection from family, abandonment from friends that were supposed to have had my back, pain in my heart from all the broken relationships - I could not afford to let go of my control.

www.ingramcontent.com/pod-product-compliance
Lightning Source LLC
Chambersburg PA
CBHW071317110426
42743CB00042B/2695